The Easter Story

This book belongs to:

_____

HARVEST HOUSE PUBLISHERS
EUGENE, OREGON

The city of Jerusalem was packed with people who had come to celebrate the Passover Festival. It was also time for Jesus to start the last stage of his life.

Jesus entered Jerusalem riding on a humble donkey. His followers threw their cloaks or large palm leaves onto the dusty ground in front of him. There was an enormous crowd because many people had heard of the miracles Jesus had preformed.

The crowd used two different items to protect Jesus from the dusty ground. Can you find the correct stickers?

cloak

palm leaf

The crowd gave Jesus a king's welcome and called out, "Hosanna to the Son of David! Blessed is he who comes in the name of the Lord!"

Jesus rode to Jerusalem on an animal. Can you find the correct sticker?

camel donkey horse

Jesus was sad because he knew that soon these people cheering would turn against him. They expected him to fight with them against the Romans, and that was not what he was on earth to do.

It was nearly time for the Passover feast, and a kind man had set aside a room for the disciples to prepare for it.

Can you find the stickers for the items Jesus used to clean the disciples' feet?

towel

That night while they were eating, Jesus filled a basin full of water and began to wash the disciples' feet like a servant.

The disciples were speechless, but when Jesus tried to wash Simon Peter's feet, Simon Peter protested and said, "Lord, you mustn't wash my feet!"

Jesus replied gently, "You don't understand what I am doing, but later it will be clear to you." Jesus had washed their feet so they could learn to do the same for each other one day.

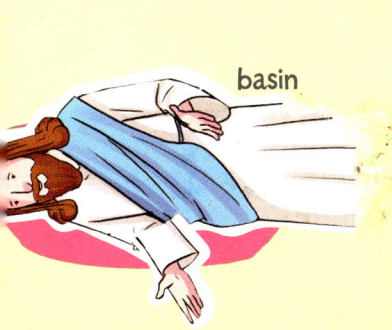
basin

jug of water

Jesus knew he would soon have to leave his friends. "Soon one of you will betray me," he said. After hearing Jesus' words, the disciples were in shock.

Even though Judas Iscariot left the room, the other disciples did not know that he was the traitor and would betray Jesus by telling Jesus' enemies where to find him that same night—in exchange for thirty silver coins.

Jesus used objects to represent his body and his blood. Can you find the stickers for these objects?

grapes

bread

Jesus passed around bread to represent his body and wine to represent his blood before telling the disciples he was going to leave them.

After Jesus told them this, Simon Peter protested, but Jesus answered, "You will disown me three times before the cock crows!" Peter was horrified. He did not believe this could ever happen!

wine

jug

Jesus had been praying quietly in the Garden of Gethsemane when a crowd of armed people burst into the garden. Judas had brought them here to arrest Jesus.

Jesus allowed the men to arrest him by saying, "I am the one you have come to find. Let the others go. You didn't need to come here with swords and clubs."

All the disciples fled, except Simon Peter, who followed the soldiers to a courtyard where he waited with the guards. Suddenly one of the servants saw him and said, "Weren't you with Jesus?"

Here are some animals. Which animal showed Simon Peter's betrayal to Jesus?

crow   parrot